A Constitutional Faith *is a revised version of a series of three lectures delivered at the Columbia University School of Law in the James S. Carpentier Series by Hugo LaFayette Black in March of 1968. These lectures were the twenty-second in a series established in 1903 by General Horace W. Carpentier of the Class of 1848 Law in honor of his brother. General Carpentier expressed the desire that the lecturers be "chosen for pre-eminent fitness and ability" and that "this lectureship will be made so honorable that nobody, however great or distinguished, would willingly choose to decline your invitation."*

Previous lectures in this series have been given by

1904–5	*James Bryce, Viscount Bryce*
1907–8	*John Chipman Gray*
1910–11	*Arthur Lionel Smith*
1910–11	*David Jayne Hill*
1911–12	*Sir Frederick Pollock*
1913–14	*Sir Courtenay Ilbert*
1916–17	*Harold Dexter Hazeltine*
1919–20	*Willard Barbour*
1923–4	*Sir Paul Vinogradoff*
1926–7	*Sir William Searle Holdsworth*
1927–8	*Benjamin Nathan Cardozo*
1940–1	*Sir Cecil Thomas Carr*
1955	*Edmund Morris Morgan*
1955	*Thomas Reed Powell*
1956	*Glanville Llewelyn Williams*
1962	*Edwin Wilhite Patterson*
1963	*Elliot Evans Chealtham*
1965	*Leon Radzinowicz*
1966	*Benjamin Kaplan*
1967	*Adolph Augustus Berle*

A CONSTITUTIONAL FAITH

A CONSTITUTIONAL FAITH

Hugo LaFayette Black 1886 — 1971

ASSOCIATE JUSTICE, SUPREME COURT
OF THE UNITED STATES

with a foreword by **WILLIAM C. WARREN**

ALFRED · A · KNOPF

New York · 1968

THIS IS A BORZOI BOOK
PUBLISHED BY ALFRED A. KNOPF, INC.

FIRST EDITION

Contents

I   THE ROLE OF THE COURTS IN OUR
        CONSTITUTIONAL SYSTEM   /3

II   DUE PROCESS OF LAW   /23

III   THE FIRST AMENDMENT   /43

EPILOGUE   /64

TABLE OF CASES   /i

INDEX   /v

[v]

*This book is dedicated to my Mother,
my wife Josephine, my wife Elizabeth,
and my daughter Josephine.*

Foreword

by William C. Warren

In these days of impatient and impassioned discussion it is indeed reassuring to hear a voice speak with calm incisiveness of the certainties of life. This is especially true when the voice is that of a public servant such as Mr. Justice Black.

In these James S. Carpentier lectures delivered at the Columbia University School of Law, Mr. Justice Black sets forth what he characterizes as a confession of his articles of constitutional faith. Drawing upon his study, reflection, and experience as a citizen, lawyer, police court judge, prosecuting attorney, senator, and justice of the Supreme Court, Mr. Justice Black reaffirms his belief in his "legal bible," the Constitution of the United States, and discusses the interpretive role of the Supreme Court.

He reiterates his lifelong convicton that the courts should always try to follow faithfully the true meaning of the Constitution and other laws as actually written, leaving to Congress changes in its statutes, and leaving the problem of adapting the Constitution to meet new needs to constitutional amendments approved by the people under constitutional procedures. The meaning of the labels "judicial activism" and "judicial restraint" is examined and discussed in detail. Mr. Justice Black explains his view that the Due Process Clause of the Fourteenth Amendment has the effect of making the entire Bill of Rights applicable to the states. Finally, he speaks of the indispensable safeguards of the First Amendment, especially in what he conceives to be its absolute guarantee of freedom of speech, press, and peaceful assembly. He carefully distinguishes conduct not protected by the First Amendment, such as picketing or demonstrating, even though utilized to communicate ideas. The First Amendment, in his view, does not guarantee that people can, wholly regardless of the rights of others, go where they please and when they please to argue for their views; such conduct may be regulated.

Mr. Justice Black has now been on the Supreme Court for thirty years—a record that only eight justices other than himself have achieved. In this period he has had the satisfaction of seeing many of his dissenting views of earlier years become the law of the land. Always a vigorous champion, he continues to press his views upon the court and to influence strongly its decisions. Time is wiser than man, and I am sure that when the judicial history of this period is written, Mr. Justice Black will be found to have played an outstanding and commanding role in the development of the law.

Success gives one great satisfaction. In this instance, Mr. Justice Black's charming wife, Elizabeth Black, and I successfully conspired to get him to break his long-standing rule of not speaking out on constitutional issues. These lectures represent an exceedingly rare extrajudicial appearance and for that reason have great scholarship value to students of constitutional law.

WILLIAM C. WARREN
July 8, 1968   *Dean of the Faculty of Law*
Columbia University

Preface

Over ten years ago I promised Dean Warren that I would deliver the Carpentier Lectures at some conveniently distant future time. After continuous pursuit, that promise and Dean Warren finally caught up with me. Since I usually refuse such offers you might be interested to learn how I happened to make the promise in the first place. The Dean's proficient espionage corps in some unaccountable way unearthed the well-guarded secret that my wife and I hit tennis balls occasionally—that is every day when she and the weather permit. The Dean then indicated to me that he and Mrs. Warren would like to challenge Mrs. Black and me to a match, and we promptly invited them to our home in Virginia to play tennis and have dinner with us. At that time, knowing full well what the Dean was after, I had the firmest intention to decline to deliver these lectures. But fate was not to permit it. My wife had just begun to play tennis and her aim was anything but accurate. Up to the afternoon of our match with the Warrens no person on the other side of a tennis net could possibly have been in danger from the balls which, when she touched them at all, slid harmlessly off the wooden part of her racket. That afternoon, however, she, for the first time in her life, hit a ball solidly and forcefully, squarely in the middle of her racket strings. It sailed away apparently as fast and as hard as a Babe Ruth home run or a Don Budge backhand, landing squarely in the Dean's eye! Neither a mint julep, like the Dean was brought up on in Texas, nor a juicy, tender, well-broiled steak, would cure that eye. Like the Prophet's gourd, it just "kep' on growin." With that swollen eye glued on me he proceeded after dinner to tell me *again* and *again* and *again* that this country and indeed the world, and certainly he, would never be quite the same unless I made these Carpentier Lectures. Under the circumstances, I capitulated, and appeared over ten years later— which some critics of the legal profession would say is about as fast as a lawyer ever does anything. As things have turned out, I think perhaps it is fortunate that I gave the lectures in 1968 in light of current comments that I have changed my views, with the implication that I am now deciding constitutional issues differently from the way I would have several years ago.

A series of speakers have appeared at Columbia from time to time during the past half century to deliver the Carpentier Lectures. The lectures are so named because in 1903 General Horace W. Carpentier, an 1848 Columbia graduate, made a generous financial grant to his alma mater to provide in the Columbia Law School "a special course of lectures on the science of law . . . by some one chosen for preeminent fitness and ability." Lectures previous to mine have been delivered by an exceedingly distinguished line of scholars and teachers among whom were Lord Bryce, Professor William S.

Holdsworth, Sir Frederick Pollock, and our own gentle and great jurist Mr. Justice Cardozo. It is needless for me to say that I was highly honored, and indeed a little awed, to be associated with such a pre-eminent group of legal scholars and philosophers.

My intention in delivering the lectures was to describe, in as simple and clear language as I could use, my constitutional faith. After more than thirty years on the Supreme Court, I am convinced that the basic tenets of this faith have not changed. In saying this I do not deny that I have on occasion reversed myself. A clear example of this was my vote with the majority in *West Virginia State Board of Education* v. *Barnette*, 319 U. S. 624 (1943), which overruled *Minersville School District* v. *Gobitis*, 310 U. S. 586 (1940), and held that a state law requiring school children, contrary to their religious faith, to salute the flag and recite the pledge of allegiance violated the First and Fourteenth Amendments to the Constitution. I had voted with the Court in upholding such a law in the earlier *Gobitis* case. Reluctance to make the federal Constitution a rigid bar against state regulation of conduct thought inimical to the public welfare was the controlling influence that caused me to consent to the *Gobitis* decision. Long reflection convinced me that although the principle was sound, its application in the particular case was wrong, and I clearly stated this change of view in a concurring opinion in *Barnette* which Justice Douglas joined. Life itself is change and one who fails to recognize this must indeed be narrow-minded; thus I make no apology for such changes as are illustrated by the *Barnette* case, where, I might add, I took pains to point out just what I was doing. But this type of change is one thing and a change in basic constitutional philosophy is another. I think that I can say categorically that I have not changed my basic constitutional philosophy—at least not in the last forty years. And it is about this constitutional philosophy that I wish to write in this book.

In these pages I shall discuss specifically "judicial activism," "judicial restraint," "due process of law," and First Amendment rights. In all that I write I shall emphasize my reasons for believing (probably contrary to what you have heard) that the courts should always try faithfully to follow the true meaning of the Constitution and other laws as actually written, leaving to Congress changes in its statutes, and leaving the problem of adapting the Constitution to meet new needs to constitutional amendments approved by the people under constitutional procedures.

In agreeing to deliver the Carpentier Lectures I was not unaware that many good people think that judges, more particularly Supreme Court justices, should never discuss legal questions beyond the requirements of particular cases which come before them. But in a country like ours, where the people have a voice in their government, public lectures about the Constitution and government can doubtless stimulate, and even help to clarify, discussion of vital constitutional issues that face our society. Under these circumstances I cannot say that judges should be completely disqualified from participating in such discussions. In fact, some of the Supreme Court's ablest and most esteemed members have given lectures and written essays and comments on legal subjects, many of which have proven of great benefit and profit to law students, lawyers, and judges, as well as to the development and understanding of our Constitution and of the law in general. To mention only a few, one thinks immediately of Justices Wilson, Story, Miller, and the first Justice John Marshall Harlan. The advantage of such lectures to an individual justice is that he has an opportunity to talk about his constitutional views with more range than he can in written opinions in particular cases. In this way he may be able to give a coherence and clarity not otherwise present in views scattered throughout his written Court opinions. I am unable to say that such a result is not desirable.

For reasons that are persuasive to me, growing out of my study, reflection, and experience as a citizen, a lawyer, a police court judge, a prosecuting attorney, a senator, and a justice of the Supreme Court, I have reached my views. I fully realize that many highly capable, sincere, patriotic people have in the past disagreed with these views, many disagree with them now, and many more will disagree with them in the future. My purpose here is not to argue with or to answer any of those who do disagree, to question their motives, or to reflect upon their candor, their intelligence, or their judgment. My object, rather, is to state, in a way that can be understood, some of my own beliefs and some reasons for them, concerning a number of controversial, constitutional questions. And of course it is entirely too late in my life to say things I do not believe.

A CONSTITUTIONAL FAITH

I

THE ROLE OF THE COURTS IN OUR CONSTITUTIONAL SYSTEM

IT IS OF PARAMOUNT IMPORTANCE TO ME THAT OUR COUN-try has a written constitution. This great document is the unique American contribution to man's continuing search for a society in which individual liberty is secure against governmental oppression. And I am proud to say that since it was written and signed in 1787, our Constitution has been a model for other experiments around the globe where men have attempted to establish governments controlled by the people themselves.

The American Constitution is no accident of history, but is the evolutionary product of man's striving throughout past ages to protect himself from tyrannical kings, potentates, and rulers. For example, we find influences even from the Roman period as shown by the following passage of a letter from Trajan to Pliny: "Anonymous informations ought not to be received in any sort of prosecution. It is introducing a very danger-ous precedent, and it is quite foreign to the spirit of our age."[1] At about the same period Festus rebuked those

[1] 9 Harvard Classics, 428 (1909).

who asked that Paul be convicted upon secret information in this way: "It is not the manner of the Romans to deliver any man to die before that he which is accused have the accusers face to face, and have license to answer for himself concerning the crime laid against him."[2] Both of these passages contain the seed of our constitutional right to confront those who accuse us. It is true that there were many subsequent periods of history in which these and similar noble expressions were completely disregarded, but nevertheless they were a part of the tradition of learning of those men like the Founders of our nation who were students of the classical period.

Although other traditions were important, there can be no doubt that knowledge of the English experience influenced our Founding Fathers most in adopting the Constitution. They were familiar with the terrible use of bills of attainder, such as the one promulgated in Ireland during the brief reign there of deposed James II of England. This bill condemned to exile or death literally thousands of people without a trial and without even a chance to discover if they were attainted until too late to do anything about it.[3] The Framers were familiar with pleas for counsel like that of John Lilburne, the contentious Puritan dissenter, who, during his trial for treason in 1649, told the court: "I again humbly desire to have counsel assigned to me to consult with, what these formalities in law signify; so that I may not throw away my life ignorantly upon forms."[4] When refused counsel by

[2] Acts 25:16.

[3] See the appendix to my concurring opinion in *Joint Anti-Fascist Refugee Committee* v. *McGrath,* 341 U. S. 123, 146–149 (1951).

[4] Lilburne (Treason Trial 1649) 4 Howell's State Trials, 1294 (1809).

the court, Lilburne again pleaded: "And now, Sir, I again desire counsel to be assigned to me, to consult with in point of law, that so I may not destroy myself through my ignorance."[5] Lilburne finally concluded: "For my part, Sir, I must look upon myself as a lost and dead man, if I have not counsel to help my ignorance, to pitch upon those things that tend to my preservation. And therefore if you will not assign me counsel to advise and consult with, I am resolved to go no further, though I die for it; and my innocent blood be upon your heads!"[6] Also, many of the Framers were familiar with the importance of the privilege against self-incrimination, as the Supreme Court recognized in the case of *Brown* v. *Walker,* 161 U. S. 591, 597, decided in 1896. The Court there referred to the seditious libel trial of the Puritan preacher John Udall, who declared to the court trying him: "I will take an oath of allegiance to her majesty, wherein I will acknowledge her supremacy according to statute, and promise my obedience as becometh a subject; but to swear to accuse myself or others, *I think you have no law for it.*"[7] And finally many of the Framers knew about the earlier periods of English history where trials for *state offenses* "were a mere mockery of justice, being, in fact, only employed by the government as a means of destroying obnoxious individuals, with sufficient pomp and circumstances to hold the multitude in awe."[8] Because of this knowledge of the English experience and legal history the Founders of our country wrote into the Constitution prohibitions

---

[5] Lilburne, *supra.*

[6] Lilburne, *supra,* 1306.

[7] Trial of Udall (1590) 1 Howell's State Trials, 1275 (1816) (emphasis added) .

[8] Jardine, 1 *Criminal Trials,* 8 (1832) .

against bills of attainder, trials without counsel, self-incrimination, and other evils expressly enumerated which commonly are practiced by tyrannical governments.

I must mention also the influence of the Levellers, that band of Puritan reformers who spoke out against the excesses of their own faith as well as others. Their proposal of *An Agreement of the Free People of England*, if adopted, would have become a written constitution for it contained the following clause: "Besides, that which is done by one Parliament, as a Parliament, may be undone by the next Parliament: but an Agreement of the People begun and ended amongst the People can never come justly within the Parliaments [*sic*] cognizance to destroy."[9] In this and so many other provisions providing protections for the people against governmental interference with their lives, liberties, and properties the Levellers' Agreement clearly foreshadowed our own Constitution.

Lastly, a critically important factor in considering the basic purpose of the Constitution is the disappointing experience of the thirteen new states under the Articles of Confederation. Each state had been too jealous of its own power to give enough authority to the national government to form a unified country. Men like Washington, Jefferson, Madison, Hamilton, and Adams saw this weakness in the Articles and knew that a national government with sufficient powers to protect and defend itself had to be established if a real country was to be created. The instrument they and others used to form this country was our written Constitution. A written

[9] Frank, *The Levellers*, 182 (1955).

constitution was chosen not only because some sort of mutual agreement among the states was necessary, but also because this was the best way to protect minority rights from the tyranny of the majority. Even the original protections of the Constitution were not considered enough, and Madison urged the adoption of a group of Amendments, known as our Bill of Rights, in the following language:

> It will be a desirable thing to extinguish from the bosom of every member of the community, any apprehensions that there are those among his countrymen who wish to deprive them of the liberty for which they valiantly fought and honorably bled. . . . There is a great body of people falling under this description, who at present feel much inclined to join their support to the cause of Federalism, if they were satisfied on this one point. We ought not to disregard their inclination, but . . . expressly declare the great rights of mankind secured under this Constitution. . . . [T]he great object in view is to limit and qualify the powers of Government, by excepting out of the grant of power those cases in which the government ought not to act, or to act only in a particular mode.[1]

I must point out here the distinction Madison drew between those areas where government was not to act at all and those areas where it was to act only in a particular manner. This will be a crucially important distinction when I discuss my view of the absolute command of the First Amendment in the third chapter.

I have inserted this brief historical résumé because I am discussing my constitutional faith and that faith has

[1] Vol. 1, *Annals of Congress,* 1st Cong., 1789–90, p. 432 & p. 437.

in many ways been fashioned and shaped by my reading of the historical events bearing on our Constitution. For example, I strongly believe that this history shows that the basic purpose and plan of the Constitution is that the federal government should have no powers except those that are expressly or impliedly granted, and that no department of government—executive, legislative, or judicial—has authority to add to or take from the powers granted it or the powers denied it by the Constitution. Our written Constitution means to me that where a power is not in terms granted or not necessary and proper to exercise a power that is granted, no such power exists in any branch of the government—executive, legislative, or judicial. Thus, it is language and history that are the crucial factors which influence me in interpreting the Constitution—not reasonableness or desirability as determined by justices of the Supreme Court. For as the Supreme Court said in 1887 in *Ex Parte Bain,* 121 U. S. 1, 12: "It is never to be forgotten that, in the construction of the language of the Constitution . . . as indeed in all other instances where construction becomes necessary, we are to place ourselves as nearly as possible in the condition of the men who framed that instrument."

Of course I realize "that it is *a constitution* we are expounding." But this does not mean that in order to obtain results thought to be desirable at the time, judges may rewrite our basic charter of government under the guise of interpreting it. This view which I have of the Constitution does not render government powerless to meet new times, new circumstances, and new conditions. And I think that is exemplified most clearly by the Commerce Clause which gives Congress the broad, general power to regulate commerce. The fact that railroads or automobiles were unknown to the Framers does not mean that the power granted by the Constitution does not apply to them, for Congress is given power to regulate *all commerce,* and it makes no difference whether that commerce is carried on by ox wagons or jet planes. In construing a specific constitutional provision, such as the Commerce Clause, I willingly go as far as that provision can be taken. This is illustrated by my opinion for the Court in *U. S.* v. *Southeastern Underwriters Association,* 322 U.S. 533 (1944), which held for the first time that the Commerce Clause grants to Congress the power to regulate insurance transactions stretching across state lines. But I refuse to go farther than a specific provision can be taken under the Necessary and Proper Clause. Thus, as I made clear recently in my dissent in *Griswold* v. *Connecticut,* 381 U. S. 479, 507 (1965), I can find in the Constitution no language which either specifically or implictly grants to all individuals a constitutional "right of privacy." There are, of course, guarantees in certain specific constitutional provisions which are written in part so that they protect privacy at certain times and places with respect to certain activities. But, even though I like my privacy as well as the next person, I am nevertheless compelled to admit that the states have a right to invade it unless prohibited by some specific constitutional provision. For this reason I could not find the Connecticut contraception law unconstitutional. Similarly, in the case this term of *Katz* v. *United States,* 389 U. S. 347, 364 (1967), I simply could not find that the words of the Fourth Amendment

prohibiting unreasonable searches and seizures also pro-
hibit eavesdropping. Fully realizing that an argument
based on the meaning of words lacks the scope, and no
doubt the appeal, of broad policy discussions and philosophical discourses on such nebulous subjects as privacy,
I just cannot say that a conversation may be "searched"
or "seized" within the ordinary and generally accepted
meanings of those words. When this is reinforced by the
historical evidence that the Framers were aware of the
practice of eavesdropping, which is mentioned even in
Blackstone's *Commentaries,* I cannot help but believe
that if they had desired to outlaw or restrict the use of
evidence obtained by such a practice, they would have
used the appropriate language in the Fourth Amendment to do so.

I am well aware of the criticisms leveled against me
that I try to follow the literal meanings of words and
look too much to the history of the Constitution and the
debates surrounding its adoption and the adoption of
the Fourteenth Amendment. And I realize that in following this procedure in many recent cases I have
reached results which many people believe to be undesirable. This has caused a new criticism to spring up that
I have now changed my views. But I assure you that in
attempting to follow as best I can the Constitution as it
appears to me to be written, and in attempting in all
cases to resist reaching a result simply because I think it
is desirable, I have been following a view of our government held by me at least as long as I have been a lawyer.
This view is based on my belief that the Founders wrote
into our Constitution their unending fear of granting
too much power to judges. Such a fear is perhaps not

so prevalent today in certain intellectual circles where the judiciary is generally held in high esteem for changes which it has made in our society which these people believe to be desirable. Many of these changes I believe were constitutionally required and thus I wholeheartedly support them. But there is a tendency now among some to look to the judiciary to make all the major policy decisions of our society under the guise of determining constitutionality. The belief is that the Supreme Court will reach a faster and more desirable resolution of our problems than the legislative or executive branches of the government. To the people who have such faith in our nine justices, I say that I have known a different court from the one today. What has occurred may occur again. I would much prefer to put my faith in the people and their elected representatives to choose the proper policies for our government to follow, leaving to the courts questions of constitutional interpretation and enforcement. Just to show that such a view is not a new one, I would like to quote a statement of mine made during a speech in 1937 when I was a member of the United States Senate and to which I still wholeheartedly subscribe:

> Most of the framers believed in popular government by the people themselves. Like Jefferson they were not willing to trust lifetime judges with omnipotent powers over governmental policies. They were familiar with the lessons of history, and they knew that the people's liberty was safest with the people themselves or their properly elected representatives. They knew that their English ancestors had fought for their liberties through their legisative repesentatives, and that they were too often compelled to wage

battle against the combined powers of the judges and the king.[2]

Part of the argument in favor of a judiciary restrained only by its own ideas of right and wrong is the phrase with which I am sure the reader is familiar, that "liberty is secure while this Court sits." The trouble with this argument is that liberty, at least as I read it defined by the Bill of Rights, has not always been secure while the Supreme Court was sitting. For example, the Supreme Court upheld Illinois in preventing a man from practicing law because of deeply held religious convictions against killing other human beings in time of war (*In re Summers*, 325 U. S. 561 [1945]); it sanctioned for many years denial of counsel in criminal cases (*Betts* v. *Brady*, 316 U. S. 455 [1942], *Foster* v. *Illinois*, 332 U. S. 134 [1947]); it refused even to allow judicial inquiry into the deportation of allegedly dangerous aliens (*Ludecke* v. *Watkins*, 335 U. S. 160 [1948]), and it failed to strike down political test oaths against communism as a requirement of labor union officers (*American Communications Association* v. *Doud*, 339 U. S. 382 [1950]). Power corrupts, and unrestricted power will tempt Supreme Court justices just as history tells us it has tempted other judges. For, unfortunately, judges have not been immune to the seductive influences of power, and given absolute or near absolute power, judges may exercise it to bring about changes that are inimical to freedom and good government. In this context I cannot help recalling the Ship Money cases during the reign of Charles I of England when a majority of judges

[2] 8 *Congressional Record,* Appendix 306 (1937).

[12]

could always be counted on to give Charles a free rein to collect money through the device of the Ship Money Tax although Charles was going against the clear law of Parliament. And anyone familiar with English history knows of many other flagrant abuses by judges, usually carried out so as to make sure that the Crown got its way. In this connection I must mention that delightful poem by John Wilkes, who established *The North Briton* political newspaper in 1762:

> With palsy'd hand, shall justice hold the scale
> And o'er a judge, Court Complaisance prevail;
> Satire's strong dose the malady requires.
> I write—when lo! the Bench indignant fires;
> Each hoary head erects its load of hair,
> Their furs all bristle, and their eye-balls glare.
> In rage they roar. With rev'rend ermine sport!
> "Seize, seize him, tipstaff!—Tis Contempt of Court."[3]

Wilkes later published issue No. 45 of his newspaper which the King considered an insult to the Crown. Wilkes was arrested, committed to the Tower, held incommunicado without the right to counsel, and his house was ransacked for papers. A controversy thus began which lasted for years. The colonists were so incensed over this treatment of Wilkes that in South Carolina No. 45 was republished, and in Charleston, Club No. 45 of the Friends of Liberty was organized. A liberty tree was decorated with 45 lights, 45 rockets were fired and a procession, preceded by 45 lights, marched to the banquet hall which was lighted with 45 candles, and on the table were 45 punch bowls. In 1769 the South Carolina House of Commons, by resolution, instructed

[3] *The North Briton,* Saturday, November 12, 1768.

[13]

the treasurer to remit 1,500 pounds to England to aid Wilkes in his contest.[4] I think these historical events graphically illustrate the kind of awareness of past English practices which led to the adoption of our Constitution with its Bill of Rights' safeguards against excessive legislative, executive, or judicial power.

Judges may also abuse power, of course, not because they are corrupt, but because of a completely honest belief that unless they do act the nation will suffer disaster. Unfortunately such honest beliefs too often reflect nothing more than an all-too-common human hostility to change. Other judges, with an equally honest belief that changes are absolutely imperative, take it upon themselves to make changes which Congress alone has legislative power to make. Thus, for the reasons that I have described, I strongly believe that the public welfare demands that constitutional cases must be decided according to the terms of our Constitution itself and not according to the judges' views of fairness, reasonableness, or justice. This will be dealt with in greater detail in the chapter on due process. Because of my ultimate faith in the people and their representatives, I have no fear of constitutional amendments properly adopted, but I do fear the rewriting of the Constitution by judges under the guise of interpretation.

With what I have written in mind, I would next like to discuss a name which of late years has crept into our vocabulary and which has frequently been applied to me: "judicial activist." In the main this term has been used as one of criticism and reproach aimed at federal judges, particularly justices of the United States Su-

[4] Patterson, *Free Speech and a Free Press*, 59–64 (1939).

preme Court, who, in deciding cases before them, are charged with either (1) being willing or even anxious to determine constitutional questions that could have been avoided or (2) determining constitutional and other legal questions not on the basis of what the law is but on what the deciding judges believe it should be. Since this name "activist" has been applied to me as a label, which unfortunately I think has served as a substitute for careful thinking and writing and also as a fallacious short cut to unjustified conclusions, I would like, so to speak, to set the record straight.

There is one school of legal thought that seems to rest on the premise that it is an unpardonable constitutional sin for a judge to decide a case on a constitutional ground if there is any possible excuse either to refuse to decide it at all or to decide it on some statutory or other nonconstitutional ground. A violation of this *judge-created* judicial offense is often given the bad sounding label of "judicial activism" and the judge who commits the sin is branded an "activist." I cannot myself subscribe to the view that judges should always and invariably avoid a determination of constitutional questions if it is in any way possible to dispose of a particular case on a nonconstitutional ground. There are few cases, if any, where judges cannot conjure up and articulate arguments that are at least plausible to get rid of cases on nonconstitutional grounds. Such a resort to merely plausible reasons to avoid deciding constitutional questions has never seemed to me to be an ennobling example of judicial piety, morals, or ethics. The necessity for complete candor in deciding cases cannot, in my opinion, be outweighed by any supposed dogmatic imperative to avoid constitutional questions. There come times when the public welfare calls loudly for putting an end to constitutional doubts about laws that may vitally affect the daily lives and practices of millions of people. Such doubts about highly valuable constitutional or statutory rights may cause delays in their enjoyment tantamount to their complete destruction. And persons subjected to burdensome duties by new untested statutes frequently may be caused to suffer irreparable losses by dilatory judicial practices that prevent constitutional tests of those new laws in the courts.

A good example of this kind of thing is the statute establishing the Subversive Activities Control Board. This is a law, which, as I stated in my dissenting opinions in *Communist Party* v. *Subversive Activities Control Board,* 367 U. S. 1, 137 (1961), and *American Committee for Protection of Foreign Born* v. *Subversive Activities Control Board,* 380 U. S. 503, 511 (1965), is a bill of attainder; imposes cruel, unusual, and savage punishments for thought, speech, writing, petition and assembly; and stigmatizes people for their beliefs, associations and views about politics, law and government. And yet since 1951, when a three-judge District Court in *Communist Party* v. *McGrath,* 96 F. Supp. 47, (D. of C. 1951) refused to rule on the constitutionality of the Subversive Activities Control Act, 64 Stat. 987–1005, 50 U. S. C. §§ 781–798 (1964), important provisions of this statute have been enforced. In case after case affecting so-called Communist-front organizations the parties have been told that the crucial constitutional issue was not yet ripe. This reached what in my mind was the height of absurdity in the case of *Veterans of the Abraham Lin-*

coln Brigade v. *Subversive Activities Control Board,* 380 U. S. 513 (1965), where, after fighting their way up through the tangled web of administrative and judicial review for ten years, the petitioners' constitutional questions, when they finally reached the Supreme Court, were remanded to the lower court because of the staleness of the record. Again this term the DuBois Clubs of America attempted to challenge the constitutionality of the Subversive Activities Control Board, and you would think that after sixteen years those associations threatened by the act would finally be entitled to a decision by the Supreme Court as to just how far Congress can go in establishing a pervasive regulatory scheme in the First Amendment field of speech, assembly, and association. But once again a majority of the Court refused to meet and decide the constitutional issues. *W. E. B. DuBois Clubs of America* v. *Clark,* 389 U. S. 309 (1967). In this case there was a clear possibility that the delay involved could very well result in the disintegration of the affected organization before it could have its constitutional claims adjudicated since the pressure inherent in registering with the board had already begun to take its toll. Indeed, as the petitioners pointed out in *DuBois,* the Attorney General himself had said that "one of the major purposes of the Act" was to destroy affected organizations before administrative proceedings began and that "most groups petitioned [to register] become defunct or dissolved before action could be taken." My reaction to this is that it is an outrageous violation of our Constitution that such a board, which serves no useful function and to some extent at least appears to have become a sinecure for politically expedient appointments,

[17]

is allowed for any length of time to curtail the exercise of the First Amendment rights of speech, assembly, and association. And this has been allowed to happen because of a judge-created doctrine that it is inherently good to avoid constitutional issues.

Here another label or name comes into focus; it is "judicial restraint." For this is the term frequently applied to the doctrine of avoiding constitutional questions and leaving them up in the air as long as there is a possibility of deciding a case on other grounds. Once again I think this term is ambiguous and ill-conceived and when used in this way, it is right to say that I am no apostle of this kind of judicial restraint, although, as I have made clear earlier, I believe strongly that judges are restrained by the Constitution, and that changes in that basic charter should be made by the people and their representatives and not by judges. By avoiding constitutional issues in cases such as those concerned with the Subversive Activities Control Board and others to which I need not now refer, I think the Supreme Court abdicates the responsibility assigned it under *Marbury* v. *Madison,* 1 Cranch 137 (1803), with which I fully agree, that the judicial branch of our government has the last word in deciding whether a statute is in accord with the Constitution. As Chief Justice Marshall said there:

> The powers of the Legislature are defined and limited; and that those limits may not be mistaken, or forgotten, the Constitution is written. To what purpose are powers limited, and to what purpose is that limitation committed to writing, if these limits may, at any time, be passed by those intended to be restrained? ...

Certainly, all those who have framed written constitutions contemplate them as forming the fundamental and paramount law of the nation, and, consequently the theory of every such government must be, that an act of the legislature, repugnant to the Constitution, is void. This theory is essentially attached to a written constitution. . . .[5]

I believe that the responsibility of judicial review was fully understood by those who wrote the Constitution, and certainly by those who most carefully considered the problem. This fact is shown, I think, by the *Federalist Papers*, the records of the debates in the Constitutional Convention and in the states, and the *Annals of Congress'* report of the debates on the Bill of Rights. Madison, himself, in arguing for adoption of the Bill of Rights, stated:

> If they are incorporated into the Constitution, independent tribunals of justice will consider themselves in a peculiar manner the guardians of those rights; they will be an impenetrable bulwark against every assumption of power in the Legislative or Executive; they will be naturally led to resist every encroachment upon rights expressly stipulated for in the Constitution by the declaration of rights.[6]

I think that the Framers were right in believing that such judicial power is an essential feature of our type of free government, and I believe it ill behooves the courts to restrict their usefulness in protecting constitutional rights by creating artificial judicial obstacles to the full performance of their duty.

The essential protection of the liberty of our people

[5] 1 Cranch, 176.
[6] 1 *Annals of Congress,* 439.

should not be denied them by invocation of a doctrine of so-called judicial self-restraint. This term has been made an alluring one by its worshippers connoting noble judicial conduct, somewhat as the term "judicial activism" has been used to connote something ignoble. But, as I have tried to make clear, when judges have a constitutional question in a case before them, and the public interest calls for its decision, refusal to carry out their duty to decide would not, I think, be the exercise of an enviable "self-restraint." Instead I would consider it to be an evasion of responsibility. In sum, I think determining when a judge shall decide a constitutional question calls for an exercise of sound judical judgment in a particular case which should not be hobbled by general and abstract judicial maxims created to deny litigants their just deserts in a court of law, perhaps when they need the court's help most desperately. Consequently, if it is judicial activism to decide a constitutional question which is actually involved in a case when it is in the public interest and in the interest of a sound judicial system to decide it, then I am an "activist" in that kind of case and shall, in all probability, remain one. In such circumstances I think "judicial self-restraint" is not a virtue but an evil.

When I get to the other meaning of "judicial activist," however, namely, one who believes he should interpret the Constitution and statutes according to his own belief of what they ought to prescribe instead of what they do, I tell you at once I am not in that group. The courts are given power to interpret the Constitution and laws, which means to explain and expound, not to alter, amend, or remake. Judges take an oath to support the

Constitution as it is, not as they think it should be. I cannot subscribe to the doctrine that consistent with that oath a judge can arrogate to himself a power to "adapt the Constitution to new times." The soft phrases used to claim that power for judges have siren-like appeal. For one who has a legitimate power to interpret there is at first a certain persuasive note in the constant repetition to him that in explaining a constitution meant for the ages he should not stick to its old eighteenth-century words but substitute others to make the Constitution best serve the current generation. And there is a certain appeal in the argument that the dead should not control the living. But adherence to the Constitution as written does not mean we are controlled by the dead. It means we are controlled by the Constitution, truly a living document. For it contains within itself a lasting recognition that it should be changed to meet new demands, new conditions, new times. It provides the means to achieve these changes through the amendment process in Article V. Twenty-two amendments have been added since the Constitution was adopted, some of them with very little difficulty or delay, and I have no doubt that others will be adopted when the sound views of the people call for them.

I have discussed the role of the courts and judges in our system of government under the Constitution, a Constitution which Benjamin Franklin said he supported because "I expect no better, and because I am not sure, that it is not the best."[7] Because this Constitu-

[7] Madison, *Debates in the Federal Convention* (Vol. V—Supplementary to Elliot's *Debates*, 554 [1866]).

tion has meant so much to the life of our nation, I think it is fitting to end this chapter with Madison's report of the final minutes of the convention:

> Whilst the last members were signing, DR. FRANK-LIN [who at that time was eighty-one years old and nearing the end of his glorious career], looking towards the president's chair, at the back of which a rising sun happened to be painted, observed to a few members near him, that painters had found it difficult to distinguish, in their art, a rising from a setting sun. "I have," said he, "often and often, in the course of the session, and the vicissitudes of my hopes and fears as to its issue, looked at that behind the president, without being able to tell whether it was rising or setting; but now, at length, I have the happiness to know that it is a rising, and not a setting sun."[8]

And now, more than one hundred and eighty years later, we know that Dr. Franklin was a sound prophet.

[8] Madison, *Debates in the Federal Convention* (Vol. V—Supplementary to Elliot's *Debates,* 565 [1866]).

II

DUE PROCESS OF LAW

THE FIFTH AND FOURTEENTH AMENDMENTS EACH CON-
tain a "Due Process" Clause which provides that no
person shall be deprived of "life, liberty or property
without due process of law." The meaning of this language and how it should be applied to federal legislation as part of the Fifth Amendment and state legislation as part of the Fourteenth Amendment is the subject
of this chapter.

In the past a majority of Supreme Court justices have
on occasion used the Due Process Clause to strike down
federal and state laws which these justices found to be
"unreasonable," "arbitrary," "capricious," or "contrary
to a fundamental sense of civilized justice." The clause
has also been used to hold laws, trials, and conduct unconstitutional which are "unfair," "shock the conscience," and "offend the community's sense of fair play
and decency."

Since, as I wrote in the first chapter, the cornerstone
of my constitutional faith is a basic belief that the Constitution was designed to prevent putting too much un-
controllable power in the hands of any one or more

public officials, I cannot subscribe to such a loose interpretation of due process which in effect allows judges,
and particularly justices of the United States Supreme
Court, to hold unconstitutional laws they do not like.
For what else is the meaning of "unreasonable," "arbitrary," or "capricious"—what sort of limitations or restrictions do these phrases put on the power of judges?
What, for example, do the phrases "shock the conscience" or "offend the community's sense of fair play
and decency" mean to you? I submit that these expressions impose no limitations or restrictions whatever on
judges, but leave them completely free to decide constitutional questions on the basis of their own policy
judgments. I deeply fear for our constitutional system of
government when life-appointed judges can strike down
a law passed by Congress or a state legislature with no
more justification than that the judges believe the law is
"unreasonable."

My fear is warranted, I believe, by the decisions of an
earlier Supreme Court where a majority of the justices
used their notions of reasonableness, through the instrument of the Due Process Clause, to read their own
economic and social philosophy into the Constitution
and thwart the power of federal and state governments
to enact needed and desired changes in government policies. Once again, to show that my constitutional views
of these judicial practices have not changed, I would
like to quote from two speeches I made as a U. S. senator. On March 24, 1937, in an address in New York City,
my speech contained the following statement:

> A bare majority of the members of the Supreme
> Court of the United States have been for a number of

years assuming the right on their part to determine the *reasonableness* of State and Federal laws. [Emphasis added.] The Constitution never gave that majority any such power. The Constitution of the United States never gave to the majority of the Judges of the Supreme Court power to declare that the sovereign State of New York, with its millions of people, could not pass laws to abolish the sweatshop by providing a minimum wage or by prohibiting unduly long hours of work in industry.[1]

Of course the case I was referring to there was *Lochner* v. *New York*, 198 U. S. 45 (1905), where a majority of the Supreme Court held that a New York law, providing that no employees shall be required or permitted to work in bakeries more than sixty hours in a week, or ten hours a day, was an unreasonable, unnecessary, and arbitrary interference with an employer's liberty to buy labor and a worker's liberty to sell his labor, and thus violative of the Fourteenth Amendment. The majority in the *Lochner* case expressed its due process philosophy in the following terms:

> In every case that comes before this court, therefore, where legislation of this character is concerned and where the protection of the Federal Constitution is sought, the question necessarily arises: Is this a fair, reasonable and appropriate exercise of the police power of the State, or is it an unreasonable, unnecessary and arbitrary interference with the right of the individual to his personal liberty. . . .[2]

This test of the majority is completely contrary to my belief that the Due Process Clause does not to any ex-

---

[1] 81 *Congressional Record* Appendix 638–39 (1937).
[2] 198 U. S. 56.

tent whatever transfer to the courts the constitutional responsibility of legislatures to determine the fairness and reasonableness of laws. Of course where a specific constitutional provision, such as the Fourth Amendment, requires a court finally to determine reasonableness, then it is appropriate for a court to do so, but such action is in no way dependent on the general language of the Due Process Clause.

Justice Holmes saw through the Court's decision in *Lochner* and, correctly, I think, pointed out in his dissent the flaw in the majority opinion in that case:

> This case is decided upon an economic theory which a large part of the country does not entertain. . . . The Fourteenth Amendment does not enact Mr. Herbert Spencer's Social Statics. . . . [A] constitution is not intended to embody a particular economic theory, whether of paternalism and the organic relation of the citizen to the State or of *laissez faire*. It is made for people of fundamentally differing views, and the accident of our finding certain opinions natural and familiar or novel and even shocking ought not to conclude our judgment upon the question whether statutes embodying them conflict with the Constitution of the United States.[3]

In another speech in 1937, this time a radio address, I again had occasion to express my dismay at the Supreme Court's use of reasonableness through the Due Process Clause to paralyze legislative action to cure pressing social and economic problems. There I said:

> This judicial tinkering with the Constitution . . . told the people of Kansas [*Coppage* v. *Kansas*, 236 U. S. 1 (1915)], and also the Congress [*Adair* v. *U. S.*,

[3] 198 U. S. 75–6.

208 U. S. 161 (1908)], that our Constitution, written by lovers of freedom and liberty, prohibited a sovereign state or a sovereign nation from passing legislation to outlaw the iniquitous yellow-dog contract. It declared to the people of the Empire State that the Federal Constitution made it unlawful for them to regulate the sale of theatre tickets. [*Tyson & Brother* v. *Banton,* 273 U. S. 418 (1927)]. It has judicially declared that the great business of agriculture, even though prostrate, is not a national problem [*U. S.* v. *Butler,* 297 U. S. 1 (1936)], while bringing into its orbit of power the height of buildings, and the right to finally decree that the guarantee of a minimum living wage was beyond the scope of a democratic people in what was once the sovereign state of New York [*Lochner* v. *New York,* 198 U. S. 45 (1905)].[4]

In holding that Congress could not make it unlawful for a carrier engaged in interstate commerce to discharge an employee because of his membership in a labor organization, a majority of the Supreme Court in *Adair* stated that

the provision of the statute under which the defendant was convicted must be held to be repugnant to the Fifth Amendment and as not embraced by nor within the power of Congress to regulate interstate commerce, but under the guise of regulating interstate commerce and as applied to this case it arbitrarily sanctions an illegal invasion of the personal liberty as well as the right of property of the defendant Adair.[5]

I resurrect these old cases, the principles of which fortunately are no longer followed, to show what

[4] 81 *Congressional Record* Appendix 307 (1937).
[5] 208 U. S. 180.

judges, Supreme Court justices even, were capable of doing at one time, and to answer those people who think it proper for the Supreme Court to declare laws of Congress and the states unconstitutional when they are found to be "unreasonable," "unfair," "arbitrary," or "capricious." Justice Holmes saw this grave weakness in the open-ended due process interpretation and in his dissent from the decision forbidding New York to regulate the sale of theatre tickets wrote the following statement with which I wholeheartedly agree:

> I think the proper course is to recognize that a state legislature can do whatever it sees fit to do unless it is restrained by some express prohibition in the Constitution of the United States or of the State, and that Courts should be careful not to extend such prohibitions beyond their obvious meaning by reading into them conceptions of public policy that the particular Court may happen to entertain.[6]

Unfortunately these views expressed by Holmes have not been heeded and the Supreme Court has too often, I am afraid, adopted an interpretation of the Due Process Clause which permits judges to invalidate laws because these judges believe them to be unwise, unfair, or unreasonable. A good example of this is *Rochin* v. *California,* 342 U. S. 165 (1952). In that case, as you may remember, police officers forced a suspect to swallow a drug in order to make him vomit two capsules which turned out to contain morphine and which were admitted as evidence in his trial for a violation of the narcotic laws. A majority of the Supreme Court reversed the conviction on the ground that it was obtained by

[6] 273 U. S. 446.

methods violative of the Due Process Clause of the Fourteenth Amendment. The conduct of the officers in forcing the pills from the defendant's stomach offended due process of law, reasoned the majority, because it shocked the conscience. The majority, knowing my opposition to such a definition of due process, attempted to answer my objection as follows:

> But that does not make due process of law a matter of judicial caprice. The faculties of the Due Process Clause may be indefinite and vague, but the mode of their ascertainment is not self-willed. In each case "due process of law" requires an evaluation based on a disinterested inquiry pursued in the spirit of science, on a balanced order of facts exactly and fairly stated, on the detached consideration of conflicting claims, . . . on a judgment not *ad hoc* and episodic but duly mindful of reconciling the needs both of continuity and of change in a progressive society.[7]

The majority opinion in the *Rochin* case exemplifies in a concrete situation what I object to most in what I consider to be an unwarranted interpretation of the Due Process Clause. For the majority there held that the Due Process Clause empowers the Supreme Court to nullify any state law if its application "shocks the conscience," offends "a sense of justice," or runs counter to the "decencies of civilized conduct." Judges are to measure the validity of state practices, according to the *Rochin* opinion, not only by their reason and by the traditions of the legal profession, but by "the community's sense of fair play and decency"; by the "traditions and conscience of our people"; or by "those canons of

[7] 342 U. S. 172.

decency and fairness which express the notions of justice of English-speaking peoples." As stated in my concurring opinion, if the Due Process Clause does vest the Supreme Court with such unlimited power to invalidate laws, I am still in doubt why we should consider only the notions of English-speaking peoples to determine what are immutable and fundamental principles of justice. Moreover, one may well ask what avenues of investigation are open to discover "canons" of conduct so universally favored that the Supreme Court should write them into the Constitution. The answer in *Rochin* was that the discovery must be made by an "evaluation based on a disinterested inquiry pursued in the spirit of science, on a balanced order of facts." You may understand what this means; I do not, and yet I believe that the *Rochin* defense of the philosophy of due process which I oppose is the best one ever written to justify that philosophy. Still, however, the elaborate verbal standards offered there are to me merely high-sounding rhetoric void of any substantive guidance as to how a judge should really apply the Due Process Clause. And I cannot help but believe that most trial and appellate court judges feel the same way when they look to such opinions for guidance.

This use of the Due Process Clause has been so thoroughly discredited that the Court has recently been less willing to use it. But now there is creeping into Court opinions a willingness to hold laws unconstitutional on the same "shock the conscience" basis by invoking equal protection. (*Harper* v. *Va. Bd. of Elections,* 383 U. S. 663 [1966]) or some other clause.[8] Obviously the equal-

---

[8] See *Hood* v. *DuMonde,* 336 U. S. 535, 563–564 (1949), particularly note 14.

protection clause is no more appropriately used for a shock-the-conscience test than the Due Process Clause. The Constitution simply does not give judges any such boundless power.

Now that I have made clear my view as to what the Due Process Clause does not do, I want to explain how I think it should be interpreted and give my reasons for so thinking. I start first with the Due Process Clause of the Fifth Amendment. It should be remembered in this discussion that the Fifth Amendment, including the Due Process Clause, is a part of the Bill of Rights adopted in response to a clamor of the people that some of the original Constitution's grants of federal power were too broad and needed to be restricted. The last place in the Constitution therefore to look for more expansive grants of federal power is in that Bill of Rights. And this is as true for the federal judiciary as it is for the legislative and executive branches of government since members of all three take an oath to support the Constitution.

The Due Process Clause language has its origin in that most important Chapter 39 of the Magna Carta, which declares that "No free man shall be taken, outlawed, banished, or in any way destroyed, nor will We proceed against or prosecute him, except by the lawful judgment of his peers and by the law of the land." This chapter, as well as the others of Magna Carta, was written when the barons of England and many others had become restless, discontented, and revolutionary because of various abuses of power perpetrated by the kings and their minions. There were long, loud, and bitter protests about how the lawmaking and judicial processes were functioning. At the time of the Magna

Carta there was an uncertainty about the laws and the methods of trial that worked to deny the people equal protection of the laws. Instead of having their lives and liberty protected by a uniform "law of the land," people were liable to sudden arrest and summary conviction in courts and by so-called judicial commissions with no sure and definite procedural protections and under laws that might have been improvised to try their particular cases. It was because of these conditions that the barons at Runnymede demanded that King John sign a written guarantee that thereafter they could only have their life or liberty taken after government had moved against them in accordance with "the law of the land." I have always admired the way the Levellers stated it when several centuries later they stood on the Magna Carta and proclaimed that "A crime it cannot be, unless it be a Transgression of a Law in being, before it was committed, acted, or done; For where there is no Law, there is no Transgression."[9]

There was, of course, no intent to broaden governmental powers behind this guarantee of like procedure in all cases where government sought to punish or penalize or move its vast machinery against the citizens. What was earnestly desired was that the same kind of trials be accorded to all alike—that is, equal protection of the laws or, in the Magna Carta language, trial under the law of the land. Chapter 39 was written into the Magna Carta to secure this by requiring essentially that a trial must be before a competent tribunal that follows previously accepted procedures. No more was there to be a sentence executed on a man unless he had first been

[9] *The Leveller Tracts* (1647–53) 198 (1944).

judged guilty of some offense which the law had already established as an offense. And no more was the mere formality of legal judgment to be allowed; now there must be a genuine trial before a jury of a defendant's peers, not a hollow mockery. Then and only then would the "law of the land" be satisfied.

It has been universally acknowledged that in the Magna Carta's concept of "law of the land" is the origin of our constitutional phrase "due process of law." As Professor Dick Howard of the University of Virginia Law School has pointed out in his commentary on the Magna Carta, as early as 1354 the words "due process" were used in an English statute interpreting Magna Carta, and by the end of the fourteenth century "due process of law" and "law of the land" were interchangeable. When the English colonists settled our country they brought this expression "due process of law" with them and later quite naturally used it in the Bill of Rights' Fifth Amendment. Rooted in its Magna Carta history this term was to them a guarantee that the government would take neither life, liberty, nor property without a trial in accord with the law of the land that already existed at the time the alleged offense was committed. The Fifth Amendment Due Process Clause thus gives all Americans, whoever they are and wherever they happen to be, the right to be tried by independent and unprejudiced courts using established and nondiscriminatory procedures and applying valid pre-existing laws. There is not one word of legal history that justifies making the term "due process of law" mean a guarantee of a trial free from laws and conduct which the courts deem at the time to be "arbitrary," "unreason-

able," "unfair," or "contrary to civilized standards."
The due process of law standard for a trial is one tried
in accordance with the Bill of Rights and laws passed
pursuant to constitutional power, guaranteeing to all
alike a trial under the general law of the land.

With this important early history in mind let us now
look at the Fourteenth Amendment. In 1947, in a dissenting opinion in *Adamson* v. *California,* 332 U. S. 46,
68, I made clear my view that the Fourteenth Amendment made the Bill of Rights applicable to the states.
The reasons for this view are based on my reading of the
history of the Amendment's adoption and are stated at
length in the opinion with its attached historical appendix. In my judgment that history demonstrates that the
language of the first section of the Fourteenth Amendment, taken as a whole, was thought by most of those
responsible for its submission to the people, and by most
of those who opposed its submission, sufficiently explicit
to guarantee that thereafter no state could deprive its
citizens of the privileges and protections of the Bill of
Rights. Of course I am aware of the attacks made upon
my historical beliefs, but all I can say is that such attacks
simply have not convinced me that I am wrong. I served
in the United States Senate for ten years and believe I
have some knowledge of the legislative process. In particular I am familiar with the use of committee reports.
Applying this knowledge and experience to the legislative history surrounding the adoption of the Fourteenth
Amendment, I come to my conclusion that the purpose
of the Amendment was to make the Bill of Rights applicable to the states.

Now you can see that my interpretation of due

process is very different from the one described and challenged in the first part of this chapter. And I sincerely believe that my interpretation is much more in accord with our whole system of government under a written constitution. For in the beginning of the nation's history no one appears to have thought that due process vested power in judges to formulate rules for constitutional "fair trials." Admittedly there were a few judges who seemed to feel that they could somehow enforce a "natural law" which was over and above laws passed even in a constitutional manner, but these natural law devotees were few and far between. From the *Slaughter House Cases,* 16 Wall. 36 (1873), on through a long line of post-Fourteenth Amendment cases, the Supreme Court rejected time after time requests to adopt natural law concepts as a part of the Due Process Clause. Finally, however, the Supreme Court, in the case of *Twining* v. *New Jersey,* 211 U. S. 78 (1908), took a long step toward construing the Due Process Clause as a broad permission for courts to hold laws invalid upon their belief that the laws were unreasonable or contrary to civilized standards. This opinion, it is obvious at once, substituted the Supreme Court's definition of constitutionality for our written Constitution's carefully prescribed and limited grants of federal power. I have never been able to accept this constitutional concept. Of course the Court's duty to strike down legislative enactments which violate the Constitution requires interpretation, and since words can have many meanings, interpretation obviously may sometimes result in contraction or extension of the original purpose of a constitutional provision, thereby affecting policy. But to pass upon the constitutionality of statutes by looking to the particular standards enumerated in the Bill of Rights and other parts of the Constitution is one thing; to invalidate statutes because of application of natural law deemed to be above and undefined by the Constitution is another. In the one instance, courts proceeding within clearly marked constitutional boundaries seek to execute policies written into the Constitution; in the other, they roam at will in the limitless area of their own beliefs as to reasonableness and actually select policies, a responsibility which the Constitution entrusts to the legislative representatives of the people.

Although I assure you that I am still trying, I have never been able at any one time to get a majority of the Court to agree to my belief that the Fourteenth Amendment incorporates *all* of the Bill of Rights' provisions (the first eight Amendments to the Constitution) and makes them applicable to the states. Most of those who object to complete incorporation of the Bill of Rights point to the Seventh Amendment which guarantees a right of trial by jury in civil cases involving as much as twenty dollars. Assuming that the people might deem this or any other amendment objectionable, however, additional amendments can be adopted making the desired changes. Abolition of the Eighteenth Amendment has demonstrated the comparative ease and rapidity with which new amendments may be added. Nevertheless a majority of the Supreme Court has continued to reject the full incorporation argument. The Court has, however, moved with extreme caution in pursuing its former latitudinarian interpretation of due process and has adopted a theory of selective incorporation of different Bill of Rights' provisions. Probably the most important enunciation of this selective theory appears in *Palko* v. *Connecticut*, 302 U. S. 319 (1937), where the Supreme Court refused to hold that the Fourteenth Amendment made the double-jeopardy provision of the Fifth Amendment obligatory on the states. In so refusing, however, the Court, speaking through Mr. Justice Cardozo, was careful to emphasize that "immunities that are valid as against the federal government by force of the specific pledges of particular amendments have been found to be implicit in the concept of ordered liberty, and thus, through the Fourteenth Amendment, become valid as against the states" and that guarantees "in their origin . . . effective against the federal government alone" had by prior cases "been taken over from the earlier articles of the federal bill of rights and brought within the Fourteenth Amendment by a process of absorption."[1]

With the *Palko* case the Supreme Court adopted the principle that those Bill of Rights' provisions which are fundamental and essential to the concept of ordered liberty are made applicable to the states through the Fourteenth Amendment. While I have made it clear that I believe *all* of the Bill of Rights' provisions are made applicable to the states through the Fourteenth Amendment, I have not objected to and indeed have supported the one-at-a-time process of absorption. For as I said in 1947 in my *Adamson* dissent: "If the choice must be between the selective process of the *Palko* decision applying some of the Bill of Rights to the States, or the *Twining* rule applying none of them, I would choose the *Palko* selective process."[2]

[1] 302 U. S., at 324–325, 326.
[2] 302 U. S. at 89.

Through this process of selective incorporation the Supreme Court has held that the Fourteenth Amendment guarantees against infringement by the states the liberties of the First Amendment, the Fourth Amendment, the Fifth Amendment's privilege against self-incrimination, the Sixth Amendment's rights to notice, confrontation of witnesses, compulsory process for witnesses, and the assistance of counsel, and the Eighth Amendment's prohibition of cruel and unusual punishments. The Fifth Amendment's provision for just compensation had been applied to the states before the *Palko* decision by an essentially similar process. The best example, I think, to illustrate this movement away from the "shock-the-conscience" due process interpretation is the Self-Incrimination Clause of the Fifth Amendment. *Twining* v. *New Jersey,* which, as I have stated before, was the case where the Supreme Court took its longest step towards construing the Due Process Clause as a broad permission for courts to substitute their own notions of reasonableness for clear constitutional commands, held that the states were not bound to grant criminal defendants exemption from compulsory self-incrimination. The most significant part of this opinion is where the Court states that "it is possible that some of the personal rights safeguarded by the first eight Amendments against national action may also be safeguarded against state action, because a denial of them would be a denial of due process of law," but, and this is the critically important distinction, "[i]f this is so, it is not because those rights are enumerated in the first eight Amendments, but because they are of such a nature that they are included in the conception of due

[38]

process of law."[3] Thus the Court in *Twining* specifically rejected any connection between the Bill of Rights and the Due Process Clause. This marked the beginning of the era where due processs of law meant whatever a majority of the Supreme Court said it meant, and unfortunately, as Justice Holmes pointed out in 1930, this meant too often that judges struck down everything they thought undesirable on economic or social grounds. Finally, however, *Twining* was overruled by *Malloy* v. *Hogan,* 378 U. S. 1 (1964), which made the Fifth Amendment's prohibition against self-incrimination applicable to the states under the process of absorption which extends certain selected "fundamental" Bill of Rights' provisions to the states through the Fourteenth Amendment.

Obviously, I am not completely happy with the selective incorporation theory since it still leaves to the determination of judges the decision as to which Bill of Rights' provisions are "fundamental" and thus applicable to the states. As I said in *Adamson,* ". . . I would [prefer to] follow what I believe was the original purpose of the Fourteenth Amendment—to extend to all the people of the Nation the complete protection of the Bill of Rights. To hold that this Court can determine what, if any, provisions of the Bill of Rights will be enforced, and if so to what degree, is to frustrate the great design of a written Constitution."[4] But the selective incorporation process, as it is now being used, does limit the Supreme Court in the Fourteenth Amendment field to specific Bill of Rights' protections only

[3] 211 U. S., at 99.
[4] 332 U. S., at 89.

and keeps judges from roaming at will in their own notions of what policies outside the Bill of Rights are desirable and what are not. And it has the virtue of having worked to make most of the Bill of Rights' protections applicable to the states. For these reasons I have supported the absorption process as an alternative, although perhaps less historically supportable than complete incorporation.

I should add here that I am not bothered by the argument that applying the Bill of Rights to the states interferes with our concept of federalism in that it may prevent states from trying novel social and economic experiments. I have never believed that under the guise of federalism the states should be able to experiment with the protections afforded our citizens through the Bill of Rights. As Justice Goldberg said so wisely in his concurring opinion in *Pointer* v. *Texas,* 380 U. S. 400, 414 (1964), "to deny to the States the power to impair a fundamental constitutional right is not to increase federal power, but, rather, to limit the power of both federal and state governments in favor of safeguarding the fundamental rights and liberties of the individual. In my view this promotes rather than undermines the basic policy of avoiding excess concentration of power in government, federal or state, which underlies our concepts of federalism."

I am frequently asked what difference my view of the Due Process Clause really makes. Perhaps the best way to show it is through an example. During the campaign between Harding and Cox in 1920, President Taft wrote an article for the *Yale Review*[5] in which he stated

[5] (October 1920), Vol. X, pp. 19–20.

that the greatest domestic issue confronting the electors was whether Harding or Cox should select Supreme Court justices (it was clear that some appointments would have to be made in the near future). Taft asserted that the Democrats supported socialistic policies and would give too much power to organized labor. What the country really needed, wrote Taft, were judges who would protect the property of the people under the Due Process Clause, and Harding could be relied upon to appoint such men. Of course what President Taft really meant was that the Due Process Clause should be interpreted to mean whatever the judge construing it wanted it to mean. And what he further implied was that he wanted judges who would construe the Due Process Clause to mean what he, Mr. Taft, thought it ought to mean. Harding was elected and three new justices were appointed to the Supreme Court. As a result many 5-to-4 decisions were rendered in which the majority of justices interpreted the Due Process Clause in line with their own economic predilections. Of course I realize that you can never do away with, or indeed would I want to do away with, an individual justice's judgment. But I think there is something to our people's aspirations for a government of laws and not of men. And I cannot accept a Due Process Clause interpretation which permits life-appointed judges to write their own economic and political views into our Constitution. I earnestly believe that my due process interpretation is the only one consistent with a written constitution in that it better ensures that constitutional provisions will not be changed except by proper amendment processes.

[41]

Now you know my view as to the meaning of due process of law, as used in the Fifth and the Fourteenth Amendments. It has taken much space to explain it, but because this little phrase has become so important in our jurisprudence, I wanted to make myself absolutely clear. Let me end this chapter with the thought that it may be that those who wrote the Constitution would have done better to provide the federal courts with the power to substitute their choice of constitutional values for the choice made by the Constitution itself. Even were I able to agree that this is true, however, I still could not accept it consistently with my oath to support the Constitution. That oath means to me that I should support the Constitution as written, not as revised by the Supreme Court from time to time. And I am content to accept the Constitution as written until the people change it in the way its provisions prescribe.

III

THE FIRST AMENDMENT

THE RIGHT TO THINK, SPEAK, AND WRITE FREELY WITH-
out governmental censorship or interference is the most
precious privilege of citizens vested with power to select
public policies and public officials. To secure this privilege for the people of the United States, the First
Amendment to our federal Constitution forbids Congress (and the states through the Fourteenth Amendment) to make any law respecting or concerning the
establishment of religion, prohibiting the free exercise
of religion, abridging freedom of speech or of the press,
or of the right of the people peaceably to assemble and
petition the government for a redress of grievances. It is
because I so strongly believe that the First Amendment
freedoms are indispensable safeguards to our country's
safety and prosperity that I yielded to an irresistible
urge to make that amendment the third and last subject
of this book. The First Amendment covers too big a
field for me to discuss it exhaustively in one chapter.
Thus I will devote this chapter principally to my belief
in freedom of speech and press. But let me make it com-

pletely clear here that I stand squarely on the following statement I made, speaking for the Court, in *Everson v. Board of Education,* 330 U. S. 1 (1947), concerning the First Amendment's guarantee of religious freedom:

> Neither a state nor the Federal Government can set up a church. Neither can pass laws which aid one religion, aid all religions, or prefer one religion over another. Neither can force nor influence a person to go to or remain away from church against his will or force him to profess a belief or disbelief in any religion. No person can be punished for entertaining or professing religious beliefs or disbeliefs, for church attendance or non-attendance. No tax in any amount, large or small, can be levied to support any religious activities or institutions, whatever they may be called, or whatever form they may adopt to teach or practice religion. Neither a state nor the Federal Government can, openly or secretly, participate in the affairs of any religious organizations or groups and *vice versa.* In the words of Jefferson, the clause against establishment of religion by law was intended to erect "a wall of separation between church and state."[1]

Since the basic theme of this book is my constitutional faith, I want to explain to you my belief that the First Amendment's guarantees of freedom of speech, press, and religion are the paramount protections against despotic government afforded Americans by their Bill of Rights and that courts must never allow this protection to be diluted or weakened in any way. On the other hand, I want to emphasize that in harmony with my general views of faithful interpretation of the Constitution as written, which views I hope I have made clear in the preceding two chapters, I am vigorously opposed to

[1] 330 U. S., at 15–16.

efforts to extend the First Amendment's freedom of speech beyond speech, freedom of press beyond press, and freedom of religion beyond religious beliefs. Thus the provisions of the Amendment that make speech, press, and religion free from governmental interference do not immunize other conduct in addition to these three particularized freedoms. Likewise the provision granting the right of "peaceable assembly" should not be extended to a guarantee that people will be supplied by government or by private parties with a place to assemble even though their assembly is peaceful. With these very significant distinctions clearly in mind, I want to begin this chapter by stating what the First Amendment's guarantee of free speech means to me.

My view is, without deviation, without exception, without any ifs, buts, or whereases, that freedom of speech means that government shall not do anything to people, or, in the words of the Magna Carta, move against people, either for the views they have or the views they express or the words they speak or write. Some people would have you believe that this is a very radical position, and maybe it is. But all I am doing is following what to me is the clear wording of the First Amendment that "Congress shall make no law . . . abridging the freedom of speech or of the press." These words follow Madison's admonition that there are some powers the people did not mean the federal government to have at all. As I have said innumerable times before I simply believe that "Congress shall make no law" means Congress shall make no law. Obviously the way to communicate ideas is through words, and I believe that when our Founding Fathers, with their wisdom and patriotism, wrote this Amendment, they knew what

[45]

they were talking about. They knew what history was behind them; they were familiar with the sad and useless tragedies of countless people who had had their tongues plucked out, their ears cut off or their hands chopped off, or even worse things done to them, because they dared to speak or write their opinions. They wanted to ordain in this country that the new central government should not tell the people what they should believe or say or publish. James Madison, in explaining the sweep of the First Amendment's limitation on the federal government when he offered the Bill of Rights to Congress in 1789, is reported as having said: "The right of freedom of speech is secured; the liberty of the press is expressly declared to be *beyond the reach of this government*. . . ."[2] Thus we have the absolute command of the First Amendment that no law shall be passed by Congress abridging freedom of speech or the press. And with the passage of the Fourteenth Amendment the Supreme Court has properly recognized that this command is now as applicable against the states as it is against the federal government.

There is nothing in the language of the First Amendment to indicate that it protects only *political* speech, although to provide such protection was no doubt a strong reason for the Amendment's passage. Since the language of the Amendment contains no exceptions, I have continuously voted to strike down all laws dealing with so-called obscene materials since I believe such laws act to establish a system of censorship in violation of the

[2] (Emphasis added.) 1 *Annals of Congress,* 141 (1857) [1789–96].

[46]

First Amendment.[3] It is not difficult for ingenious minds to think up and contrive ways to escape even the plain prohibitions of the First Amendment. This same kind of ingenuity existed in the days of Rome. For example, it is said that Augustus punished people for criticizing the Emperor by the simple device of calling such criticism obscene. So far as I am concerned, I do not believe there is any halfway ground for protecting freedom of speech and press. If you say it is half free, you can rest assured that it will not remain as much as half free.

Censorship, even under the guise of protecting people from books or plays or motion pictures that other people think are obscene, shows a fear that people cannot judge for themselves. As Justice Douglas said in a dissenting opinion which I joined in *Roth* v. *United States,* 354 U. S. 476 (1957), "I have the same confidence in the ability of our people to reject noxious literature as I have in their capacity to sort out the true from the false in theology, economics, politics, or any other field."[4] And I cannot help pointing out here, in light of what seems to be happening today, that I think the Supreme Court is about the most inappropriate Supreme Board of Censors that could be found (see my dissenting opinion in *Kingsley Pictures Corp.* v. *Regents,* 360 U. S. 684, 690). We should never forget that the plain language of the Constitution recognizes that censorship

---

[3] See *Roth* v. *United States,* 354 U. S. 476, 508 (1957); *Kingsley Pictures Corp.* v. *Regents,* 360 U. S. 684, 690 (1959); *Smith* v. *California,* 361 U. S. 147, 155 (1959); *Ginzburg* v. *United States,* 383 U. S. 463, 476 (1966).

[4] 354 U. S., at 514.

is the deadly enemy of freedom and progress and forbids it.

Just as with obscenity laws, I believe the First Amendment compels the striking down of all libel laws. Thomas Jefferson indicated as much when in 1798 he made the following statement:

> [The First Amendment] thereby guard[s] in the same sentence, and under the same words, the freedom of religion, of speech and of the press, insomuch that whatever violates either throws down the sanctuary which covers the others, and that libels, falsehood and defamation, equally with heresy and false religion are withheld from the cognizance of federal tribunals. . . .[5]

Since the First Amendment has been made applicable to the states by the Fourteenth, I do not hesitate to expound the constitutional doctrine that just as it was not intended to authorize damage suits for mere words as distinguished from conduct as far as the federal government is concerned, the same rule should apply to the states. I believe with Jefferson that it is time enough for government to step in to regulate people when they *do* something, not when they *say* something. I had occasion to enunciate this view in my concurring opinion in *New York Times Co.* v. *Sullivan,* 376 U. S. 254, 293 (1964), where I voted to reverse the libel judgment "exclusively on the ground that the Times and the individual defendants had an absolute, unconditional constitutional right to publish in the Times advertisement their criticisms of the Montgomery [Ala.] agencies and officials."[6] It seems to me that under the First and Fourteenth Amendments a state has no power to use a civil libel law

[5] 8 Jefferson, *Writings* (Ford edn., 1904) , 464–5.
[6] 376 U. S., at 293.

or any other law to impose damages for merely discussing public affairs and criticizing public officials. As I said in the *Times* case, "We would, I think, more faithfully interpret the First Amendment by holding that at the very least it leaves the people and the press free to criticize officials and discuss public affairs with impunity."[7] I am aware, of course, that some writers and commentators have challenged the historical accuracy of my reading of the broad sweep of the First Amendment. But a careful review of all the evidence convinces me that my interpretation of the Amendment is accurate.

Free speech plays its most important role in the political discussions and arguments which are the lifeblood of any representative democracy. The lesson of history is crystal clear that the decline of really free political debate is one of the first signs of deterioration in an otherwise free state. Our Founding Fathers recognized this and established a system of government with its written Constitution and Bill of Rights which they believed ensured absolute freedom to any citizen to say anything and believe anything, even if that belief was contrary to our most sacred principles of government and society. Jefferson expressed it this way on the occasion of his first inauguration as President of the United States:

> If there be any among us who would wish to dissolve this Union or to change its republican form, let them stand undisturbed as monuments of the safety with which error of opinion may be tolerated where reason is left free to combat it.[8]

Unfortunately, however, the Supreme Court has refused to grant absolute protection to speech under the

[7] 376 U. S., at 296.
[8] Thomas Jefferson, First Inaugural Address, March 4, 1801.

First Amendment, as he advocated, and instead has adopted various judicial tests which are applied on a case-by-case basis to determine if the speech in question is entitled to protection. Of these the most dangerous I believe is the so-called balancing test. The Court's balancing test in effect says that the First Amendment should be read to say "Congress shall pass no law abridging freedom of speech, press, assembly and petition, unless Congress and the Supreme Court reach the joint conclusion that on balance the interest of the government in stifling these freedoms is greater than the interest of the people in having them exercised." This is closely akin to the notion that neither the First Amendment nor any other provision of the Bill of Rights should be enforced unless the Court believes it is *reasonable* to do so. This balancing test has been used to justify, among other things, the requirement that a college teacher answer questions to the House Un-American Activities Committee about alleged past Communist affiliation (*Barenblatt* v. *United States,* 360 U. S. 109 [1959]); the refusal to certify an attorney for admission to a state bar when he would not answer questions about his suspected association with Communists twenty years before (*Konigsberg* v. *State Bar,* 366 U. S. 36 [1961]); and the conviction for a crime of a defendant charged with mere membership in the Communist Party (*Scales* v. *United States,* 367 U. S. 203, [1961]).

Because of a fear of Communists these people, and others, were allowed to be punished for their political beliefs and peaceable associations. Punishment for an overt, illegal act is one thing, but punishment of a person because he says something, believes something or associates with others who believe the same thing is forbidden by the express language of the First Amendment. Yet in these cases, and too many others, people's rights are balanced away with the excuse that this country must be able to protect and preserve itself. I believe that the best way to protect and preserve the country is to keep speech and press free. No one owes his country and its form of government more than I do, and I want to see both preserved. But I believe they can be preserved only by leaving people with the utmost freedom to think and to hope and to talk and to dream if they want to dream. I do not think this government must look to force, stifling the minds and aspirations of the people. For as I said in *Barenblatt,* "no number of laws against communism can have as much effect as the personal conviction which comes from having heard its arguments and rejected them, or from having once accepted its tenets and later recognized their worthlessness."[9] Even if I did not think this, however, I could not uphold laws punishing belief in communism or in anything else because as I read the First Amendment it absolutely forbids government from outlawing membership in a political party or similar association merely because one of the philosophical tenets of that group is that the existing government should be overthrown by force at some time in the future when circumstances permit.

Not only, it seems to me, does the balancing test ignore the language of the First Amendment, but as usually applied it has an unlimited breadth which is highly dangerous. For under the balancing test the question in every case where a First Amendment right is asserted is

[9] 360 U. S., at 144.

not whether there has been an abridgment of that right, not whether the abridgment of that right was intentional on the part of the government, and not whether there was any other way in which the government could have accomplished its aim without an abridgment. Rather the question simply is whether the government has an interest in abridging the right involved and, if so, whether that interest is of sufficient importance, *in the opinion of a majority of the Supreme Court,* to justify the government's action in doing so. Such a doctrine can be used to justify almost any government suppression of First Amendment freedoms. As I have stated many times before, I cannot subscribe to this doctrine because I believe that the First Amendment's unequivocal command that there shall be no abridgment of the rights of free speech shows that the men who drafted our Bill of Rights did all the "balancing" that was to be done in this field.

In addition to balancing, the other major judicial test that has been used in the First Amendment field is that of "clear and present danger." The problem with this test is that it can be used to justify the punishment of advocacy. Thus in *Yates* v. *United States,* 354 U. S. 298 (1957), a majority of the Supreme Court said that persons could be punished for advocating action to overthrow the government by force and violence where those to whom the advocacy was addressed were urged to *do* something rather than merely *believe* in something. My objection to this approach is that under it people can still be convicted just for talking as distinguished from acting. As I said in *Yates,* "I believe that the First Amendment forbids Congress to punish people for talking about public affairs, whether or not such discussions

incites to action, legal or illegal."[1] I agree wholeheartedly with the "Statute for Religious Liberty" written by
Thomas Jefferson and passed by the Virginia Assembly
in 1785 wherein it is stated that "it is time enough for
the rightful purposes of civil government, for its officers
to interfere when principles break out into overt acts
against peace and good order. . . ."[2]

I think I have made clear my belief that the Constitution guarantees absolute freedom of speech, and I have
not flinched in applying the First Amendment to protect ideas I abhor. I have also continuously voted within
the Court to strike down all obscenity and libel laws as
unconstitutional. In giving absolute protection to free
speech, however, I have always been careful to draw a
line between speech and conduct. Thus at the very beginning of my dissent in *Beauharnais* v. *Illinois,* 343 U.
S. 250, decided in 1952, I pointed out that "The conviction rests on the leaflet's contents, not on the time, manner or place of distribution."[3] This distinction, to
which I want to devote the rest of this chapter, has been
described very well by Justice Douglas in his dissenting
opinion in *Roth* v. *United States,* 354 U. S. 476 (1957),
where he stated: "Freedom of expression can be sup-
pressed if, and to the extent that, it is so closely brigaded
with illegal action as to be an inseparable part of it."[4]

The First and Fourteenth Amendments take away
from government, state and federal, all power to restrict
freedom of speech, press, and peaceful assembly *where
people have a right to be for such purposes.* That much

[1] 354 U. S., at 340.
[2] 12 Hening's Stat. (Virginia 1823), c. 34, p. 85.
[3] 343 U. S., at 267.
[4] 354 U. S., at 514.

is clear and to me indisputable. But recently many loose words have been spoken and written about an alleged First Amendment right to picket, demonstrate, or march, usually accompanied by singing, shouting, or loud praying, along the public streets, in or around government-owned buildings, or in and around other people's property, even including their *homes,* without their owners' consent. I say these have been loose words because I do not believe that the First Amendment grants a constitutional right to engage in the conduct of picketing or demonstrating, whether on publicly owned streets or on privately owned property. The Constitution certainly does not require people on the streets, in their homes, or anywhere else to listen against their will to speakers they do not want to hear. Marching back and forth, though utilized to communicate ideas, is not speech and therefore is not protected by the First Amendment.

In order that I make myself perfectly clear on this issue, let me go into a little more detail. Picketing, demonstrating, and similar activity usually consists in walking or marching around a building or place carrying signs or placards protesting against something that has been or is being done by the person picketed. Thus a person engaged in such activities is not only communicating ideas—that is, exercising freedom of speech or press—but is pursuing a course of conduct in addition to constitutionally protected speech and press. Picketing then, as Justice Douglas pointed out in a concurring opinion which I joined in *Bakery Drivers Local* v. *Wohl,* 315 U. S. 769, 775, decided in 1942, "is more than free speech, since it involves patrol of a particular locality and since the very presence of a picket line may induce action of one kind or another, quite irrespective of the nature of the ideas which are being disseminated."[5] This is not a new idea either with me or the Supreme Court since it has long been accepted constitutional doctrine that the First Amendment presents no bar to the passage of laws regulating, controlling, or entirely suppressing such a course of marching conduct even though speaking and writing accompany it.[6] As picketing is made up of speech and press plus other conduct, so are what are popularly called demonstrations and street marches. And the conduct of demonstrators and street marchers, like that of pickets, can be regulated by government without violating the First Amendment.

It is not difficult to understand why the Founders believed that the peace and tranquillity of society absolutely compel the foregoing distinction between constitutionally protected freedom of religion, speech and press, and nonconstitutionally protected conduct like picketing and street marching. It marks the difference between arguing for changes in the governing rules of society and in engaging in conduct designed to break and defy valid regulatory laws. The cases coming before the Supreme Court involving the Mormons graphically illustrate these differences. See, for example, *Reynolds* v. *United States,* 98 U. S. 145 (1878). An important tenet of the Mormon faith is a belief in plural marriages for men. Our society, however, and most religions treat polygamy as a sinful and evil practice, one that is by

[5] 315 U. S., at 776.
[6] See *Giboney* v. *Empire Storage & Ice Co.,* 336 U. S. 490 (1949).

common consent made a crime perhaps in every state of the Union. Congress made polygamy a crime in the Territory of Utah before it became a state. When prosecuted under that law the Mormons defended on the ground that since their religious faith approved the practice, the territorial law making it a crime violated the First Amendment. The Supreme Court rejected this contention, pointing out that the First Amendment only protects the right to be a Mormon, to believe in and advocate its faith, but that a church cannot by giving conduct a religious approval bar government from making such conduct a crime. Thus the line was clearly drawn between freedom to believe in and advocate a doctrine and freedom to engage in conduct violative of law.

I had occasion to draw this same line between the constitutional right to speak and write and the nonconstitutional right to engage in the conduct of picketing in my opinion for the Court in *Giboney* v. *Empire Storage & Ice Co.*, 336 U. S. 490, decided in 1949. In that case Missouri had an antitrust, antiboycott law against combinations in restraint of trade. A union composed of ice-wagon drivers who delivered ice to homes was violently opposed to a competitive group of drivers who delivered ice to retail stores for subsequent sale to their customers. The home ice deliverers unsuccessfully tried to persuade distributors to refuse to sell ice to wagon drivers who sold to stores. The distributors could not enter into agreement to boycott the drivers who supplied the stores without violating the state's antitrust law. The home ice drivers set up pickets to march back and forth on streets adjacent to the distributors. The pickets carried placards and signs advertising the facts of their dispute with the distributors. These placards and signs were the kind of speech and press we held in *Thornhill* v. *Alabama,* 310 U. S. 88 (1940), were protected by the First Amendment. The action of the pickets in walking back and forth, however, was neither speech nor press, but conduct carried on to accomplish a boycott squarely in violation of the Missouri state law. Under these circumstances, we held that the protected speech and press did not immunize the workers' conduct in marching back and forth as pickets. In my opinion for the Court I made the following declaration: "It rarely has been suggested that the constitutional freedom for speech and press extends its immunity to speech or writing used as an integral part of conduct in violation of a valid criminal statute. We reject the contention now."[7] The opinion went on to explain that *Thornhill* v. *Alabama,* 310 U. S. 88 (1940), held the Alabama law against picketing unconstitutional not as a violation of the First Amendment, but denied enforcement because of its overbroadness and vagueness. And since *Thornhill* the Supreme Court has not even indicated that the marching element of picketing may be constitutionally protected from regulation as is speech and press.

The regulation of picketing and marching is essential since this conduct by its very nature tends to infringe the rights of others. For example, no matter how urgently a person may wish to exercise his First Amendment guarantees to speak freely, he has no constitutional right to appropriate someone else's property to do so. Our Constitution recognizes and supports the concept of private ownership of property and in the Fifth Amendment provides that "no person shall . . . be de-

[7] 336 U. S., at 498.

[57]

prived of life, liberty, or property, without due process of law; nor shall private property be taken for public use without just compensation." The long and short of this problem is that while the First Amendment does guarantee freedom to speak and write, it does not at the same time provide for a speaker or writer to use other people's private property to do so. This means that there is no First Amendment right for people to picket on the private premises of another to try to convert the owner or others to the views of the pickets.

The next question is whether the First Amendment, or any other constitutional provision, compels government, either federal or state, to provide a place for people to speak, write or assemble on government-owned streets, highways, buildings, and other publicly owned places. Certainly the language of the First Amendment provides no support for this contention. That language deals not with supplying people a place to speak, write, or assemble, but only with the right to speak, write, and assemble. It is true that the Amendment does provide that there should be no abridgment of the right to petition the government for redress of grievances. This language would unquestionably appear to require the *government* to have a place to receive petitions about grievances, but it should be noted that the petition is to be made to "government," not to the public in general. Propagandizing on the streets can hardly be the same as presenting a petition to "government" to redress grievances. Nor does a grant to the people of the right to assemble, to speak, or to write carry any inference that the government must provide streets, buildings, or places to do the speaking, writing, or assembling.

This view that I am now expressing is not a new one

with me, but one I have held for a long time. I have never doubted the power of government over its streets and public places. For example, in 1941, after I had been on the Supreme Court only a few years, I wrote a dissent in the case of *Milk Wagon Drivers Union* v. *Meadowmoor Dairies, Inc.*, 312 U. S. 287 (1941), where, although I thought the injunction against picketing was invalid because it was too broad, I nevertheless pointed out that states certainly had the power to regulate such picketing: "Furthermore," I said, "this is true because a state has the power to adopt laws of general application to provide that the streets shall be used for the purpose for which they primarily exist [travel], and because the preservation of peace and order is one of the first duties of government."[8] It is absolutely critical, however, that state regulatory laws in this area be applied to all groups alike, and these laws must never be used as a guise to suppress particular views which the government dislikes. A good example of what I mean here is the following excerpt from my concurring opinion in *Cox* v. *Louisiana,* 379 U. S. 559, 575 (1965):

> In the case before us Louisiana has by a broad, vague statute given policemen an unlimited power to order people off the streets, not to enforce a specific, nondiscriminatory state statute forbidding patrolling and picketing, but rather whenever a policeman makes a decision on his own personal judgment that views being expressed on the streets are provoking or might provoke a breach of the peace. Such a statute does not provide for government by clearly defined laws, but rather for government by the moment-to-moment opinions of a policeman on his beat. . . . This kind of statute provides a perfect device to arrest peo-

[8] 312 U. S., at 317.

ple whose views do not suit the policeman or his su-
periors, while leaving free to talk anyone with whose
views the police agree.[9]

I think there can be no doubt that the First Amendment forbids laws that open up streets, highways, and
buildings for some groups with some views, while denying their use for other groups to advocate different
views. This was an additional consideration which I
pointed out in the *Cox* case where Louisiana allowed
labor-union assembly, picketing, and public advocacy,
while denying that opportunity to groups protesting
against racial discrimination. Obviously Louisiana
could not be allowed "to pick and choose among the
views it is willing to have discussed on its streets."[1]
This, however, is not to take away from government its
necessary power to control its property, but only forbids
it to do so in a way that amounts to aiding some views,
beliefs and causes over others, which amounts to pre-
cisely the kind of governmental censorship the First
Amendment was written to proscribe.

In addition to protecting against discriminatory regulatory laws, the First Amendment prohibits a state or
municipality from regulating conduct in such a way as
to affect speech indirectly where other means are availa-
ble to accomplish the desired result without burdening
speech or where the need to control the conduct in
question is insufficient even to justify an indirect effect
on speech. Thus, as I said in *Barenblatt* v. *United States*,
360 U. S. 109 (1959), "even . . . laws governing conduct
. . . must be tested, though only by a balancing process,

[9] 379 U. S., at 579.
[1] 379 U. S., at 581.
[2] 360 U. S., at 142.

if they indirectly affect ideas."[2] A good example of what I am talking about here is the case of *Schneider* v. *Irvington,* 308 U. S. 147 (1939), which involved ordinances prohibiting the distribution of handbills in order to prevent littering. The Supreme Court forbade application of such ordinances when they affected the distribution of literature designed to spread ideas. There were other ways, we said, to protect the city from littering which would not sacrifice the right of the people to be informed. But let me make absolutely clear that this kind of balancing should be used only where a law is aimed at conduct and indirectly affects speech; a law directly aimed at curtailing speech and political persuasion can, in my opinion, never be saved through a balancing process. I should also add here that the Constitution does not require a government, either federal or state, to devote its streets, buildings, and other public places to the advocacy of causes through proscribed conduct where that government desires such facilities *uniformly* to be used only for their dedicated purposes. Of course, if a person is lawfully on the street, he carries with him his constitutional right to talk and under these circumstances his advocacy of causes may not be abridged.

From what I have said I hope it is clear that my belief is while the First Amendment guarantees freedom to write and speak, it does not guarantee that people can, wholly regardless of the rights of others, go where they please and when they please to argue for their views. Such conduct can be regulated. The streets and highways, for example, are basically dedicated to the use of travelers who wish to go from one place to another.

[2] 360 U. S., at 142.

Anything that interferes with this basic purpose interferes to a greater or lesser extent with the basic purpose of highways. Most states and municipalities, however, out of their own experience and for their own purposes, adopt on their own initiative policies that permit streets to be used on occasions for parades and marches by various groups frequently to advocate different causes. So long as this is done without discrimination against particular views such permits usually are regarded everywhere as wise procedure and as clearly within the power of a state or municipality. Mr. Justice Goldberg said as much when, in his opinion for the Court in *Cox* v. *Louisiana,* he stated:

> Nothing we have said here . . . is to be interpreted as sanctioning riotous conduct in any form or demonstrations, however peaceful their conduct or commendable their motives, which conflict with properly drawn statutes and ordinances designed to promote law and order, protect the community against disorder, regulate traffic, safeguard legitimate interests in private and public property, or protect the administration of justice and other essential governmental functions.[3]

Plainly, use of the streets for propaganda purposes can at certain times and places not only discommode travelers, but actually paralyze all use of the streets for their primary purpose, which is traveling. In these situations government must be able to regulate the offensive conduct, and I see no constitutional barrier to its doing so.

Our government envisions a system under which its policies are the result of reasoned decisions made by public officials chosen in the way the laws provide. Those laws do not provide that elected officials, council-

[3] 379 U. S., at 574.

men, mayors, judges, governors, sheriffs, or legislators, will act in response to pre-emptory demands of the leaders of tramping, singing, shouting, angry groups controlled by men who, among their virtues, have the ordinary amount of competing ambitions common to mankind. A control of this kind by such particularized groups is directly antagonistic to a control by the people's representatives chosen by them to manage public affairs. In other words, government by clamorous and demanding groups is very far removed from government by the people's choice at the ballot box. What we have in this country is a government of laws, designed to achieve justice to all, in the most orderly fashion possible, and without leaving behind a deluge of hate-breeding divisions and dangerous riots.

The First Amendment, as I have frequently said, is the heart of our Bill of Rights, our Constitution, and our nation. Where rights of communication, assembly, and protest are made secure, which is what our First Amendment is intended to do, people develop a sturdy and self-reliant character which is best for them and best for their government. This Amendment was designed and planned to give the people so great an influence over the government's affairs that our society could abandon the age-old device of settling controversies through strife which leads inevitably to hatreds and bloodshed, and substitute for strife settlements by and through the peaceful agencies of government and law. Only in this way will we as a country fulfill the promise of our Constitution to "establish Justice, insure domestic Tranquility, provide for the Common Defense, promote the general Welfare, and secure the Blessings of Liberty to ourselves and our posterity . . ."

EPILOGUE

ALTHOUGH I HAVE TOUCHED ONLY THE HIGH SPOTS OF MY
legal and constitutional views, I have rather loosely referred to what I have written as a confession of my articles of constitutional faith. And perhaps that is a fitting
description since I have discussed some of the legal and
constitutional problems around which have revolved
many of the most controversial, and, too frequently,
acrimonious discussions of the past few years. I have
tried to find and read these discussions, particularly
those challenging my own positions. Some who oppose
my views have been satisfied with efforts to destroy them
by pure logic and reason; others have added rhetoric
and emotion; still others have expressed a sort of sympa-
thy and sorrow because of the naïvety or ignorance
which alone in their judgment could account for views
with which they so violently disagree. I accept all of
such comments, however written, as honest efforts to
bring about a better administration of justice under
law. What I have written will, I trust, help in achieving
the same purpose.

I cannot close without saying a few words to express my deep respect and boundless admiration and love for our Constitution and the men who drafted it. These men met in convention at Philadelphia with instructions to do no more than amend the original Articles of Confederation. They disobeyed those instructions and came out of their convention with a document designed to unite the thirteen jealous, independent colonies into one powerful nation. By this remarkable achievement they transformed that which had been the dream of a few into a living reality. They created a government strong enough and with power enough to protect itself against its enemies, both foreign and domestic, while leaving its control to the selected representatives of free citizens themselves. I am a typical example of this highly successful experiment in government. I was born in a frontier farm home in the hills of Alabama in the troublesome times of Reconstruction, after the Civil War, and my early life was spent in plain, country surroundings. There I became acquainted with the "short and simple annals of the poor," among plain folks who learned most of their law and sound philosophies from the country schools and churches. In due course the people of Alabama chose me to be their United States senator. I served in the Senate until appointed Associate Justice of the United States Supreme Court in which position I have now served for more than thirty years. It is a long journey from a frontier farmhouse in the hills of Clay County, Alabama, to the United States Supreme Court, a fact which no one knows better than I. But this nation, created by our Constitution, offers countless examples just like mine. My experiences with and for our government have filled my heart with gratitude and devotion to the Constitution which made my public life possible. That Constitution is my legal bible; its plan of our government is my plan and its destiny my destiny. I cherish every word of it, from the first to the last, and I personally deplore even the slightest deviation from its least important commands. I have thoroughly enjoyed my small part in trying to preserve our Constitution with the earnest desire that it may meet the fondest hope of its creators, which was to keep this nation strong and great through countless ages.

Table of Cases

Adair v. *U. S.*, 208 U. S. 161 (1908), **27, 28 and** *n.*

Adamson v. *California*, 332 U. S. 46, 68 (1947), **34, 37, 39**

American Committee for the Protection of the Foreign Born v. *Subversive Activities Control Board*, 380 U. S. 503, 511 (1965), **16**

American Communications Association v. *Doud*, 339 U. S. 382 (1950), **12**

Bain, Ex Parte, 121 U. S. 1, 12 (1887), **8**

Bakery Drivers Local v. *Wohl*, 315 U. S. 769, 775 (1942), **54-5, 55***n.*

Barenblatt v. *United States*, 360 U. S. 109 (1959), **50, 51, 60 and** *n.*

Barnette, West Virginia State Board of Education v., 319 U. S. 624 (1943), **xiii**

Beauharnais v. *Illinois*, 343 U. S. 250 (1952), **53 and** *n.*

Betts v. *Brady*, 316 U. S. 455 (1942), **12**

Brown v. *Walker*, 161 U. S. 591, 597 (1896), **5**

Butler, U. S. v., 297 U. S. 1 (1936), **27**

Communist Party v. *McGrath*, 96 F. Supp. 47 (D. of C. 1951), **16**

Communist Party v. *Subversive Activities Control Board*, 367 U. S. 1, 137 (1961), **16**

Coppage v. *Kansas*, 236 U. S. 1 (1915), **26**

Cox v. *Louisiana*, 379 U. S. 559, 575 (1965), **59-60, 60***n.,* **62 and** *n.*

DuBois Clubs of America, W. E. B., v. *Clark*, 389 U. S. 309 (1967), **17**

Everson v. *Board of Education*, 330 U. S. (1947), **44 and** *n.*

Foster v. *Illinois,* 332 U. S. 134 (1947), **12**

Giboney v. *Empire Storage & Ice Co.,* 336 U. S. 490 (1949), **55***n.,* **56**

Ginzburg v. *United States,* 383 U. S. 463, 476 (1966), **47***n.*

Gobitis, Minersville School District v., 310 U. S. 586 (1940), **xiii**

Griswold v. *Connecticut,* 381 U. S. 479, 507 (1965), **9**

Harper v. *Va. Bd. of Elections,* 383 U. S. 663 (1966), **30**

Hood v. *DuMonde,* 336 U. S. 535, 562–564 (1949), **30***n.*

Joint Anti-Fascist Refugee Committee v. *McGrath,* 341 U. S. 123, 146–149 (1951), **4***n.*

Katz v. *United States,* 389 U. S. 347, 364 (1967), **9**

Kingsley Pictures Corp. v. *Regents,* 360 U. S. 684, 690 (1959), **47** **and** *n.*

Konigsberg v. *State Bar,* 366 U. S. 36 (1961), **50**

Lochner v. *New York,* 198 U. S. 45 (1905), **25, 26 and** *n.,* **27**

Ludecke v. *Watkins,* 335 U. S. 160 (1948), **12**

Malloy v. *Hogan,* 378 U. S. 1 (1964), **39**

Marbury v. *Madison,* 1 Cranch 137 (1803), **18**

Milk Wagon Drivers Union v. *Meadmoor Dairies, Inc.,* 312 U. S. 287 (1941), **59** **and** *n.*

Minersville School District v. *Gobitis,* 310 U. S. 586 (1940), **xiii**

New York Times Co. v. *Sullivan,* 376 U. S. 254, 293 (1964), **48 and** *n.,* **49 and** *n.*

Palko v. *Connecticut,* 302 U. S. 319 (1937), **37**

Pointer v. *Texas,* 380 U. S. 400, 414 (1964), **40**

Reynolds v. *United States,* 98 U. S. 145 (1878), **55**

Rochin v. *California,* 342 U. S. 165 (1952), **28, 29, 30**

Roth v. *United States,* 354 U. S. 476 (1957), **47 and** *n.*

Scales v. *United States,* 367 U. S. 203 (1961), **50**

Table of Cases

Schneider v. Irvington, 308 U. S. 147 (1939), 61

Slaughter House Cases, 16 Wall. 36 (1873), 35

Smith v. California, 361 U. S. 147, 155 (1959), 47n.

Southeastern Underwriters Association v. U.S., 322 U. S. 533 (1944), 9

Summers, In re, 325 U. S. 561 (1945), 12

Thornhill v. Alabama, 310 U. S. 88 (1940), 57

Twining v. New Jersey, 211 U. S. 78 (1908), 35, 37, 38, 39

Tyson & Brother v. Banton, 273 U. S. 418 (1927), 27

Veterans of the Abraham Lincoln Brigade v. Subversive Activities Control Board, 380 U. S. 513 (1965), 16–17

West Virginia State Board of Education v. Barnette, 319 U. S. 624 (1943), xiii

Yates v. United States, 354 U. S. 298 (1957), 52–3, 53n.

Index

Adams, John, 6
Agreement of the Free People of England, An, 6
Annals of Congress, 7n., 19 and *n.,* 46*n.*
antitrust legislation, 56
"arbitrariness" of statutes and constitutionality, 23, 24, 28, 33
Article V, 21
Articles of Confederation, 6, 65
assembly, freedom of, 16, 17, 18, 43, 45, 50, 58
association, freedom of, 17
Augustus, 47

Bill of Rights, 7, 12, 14, 19, 31, 33, 34, 36, 37, 39, 40, 44, 49, 63; *see also specific Amendments*
bills of attainder, 4, 6, 16
Blackstone's *Commentaries,* 10
boycotts, 65–7
Bryce, Lord, xiii

Cardozo, Benjamin N., xiii, 37
censorship, 47–8
Charles I, 12–13
Civil War, 65
"clear and present danger" test, 52
Club No. 45 of the Friends of Liberty, 13
Commerce Clause, 9
communism, and the First Amendment, 16–17, 50–1
Congress, U. S., 46, 56; has power to regulate all commerce, 9; legislative powers of, 14
conscientious objectors, 12
Constitution, U. S., 3 *passim;* résumé of historical events bearing on, 3–8*ff.,* 19–20
Constitutional Convention, 65
contraception law, Connecticut, 9
"contrariness to civilized justice" of statutes, and constitutionality, 23, 24, 29, 34, 35

counsel in criminal cases: denial of, 12; right to, 38
Cox, James M., 40–1
cruel and unusual punishments, prohibition of, 38

deportation of aliens, 12
double jeopardy, prohibition of, 37
Douglas, William O., xiii, 47, 53, 54
DuBois Clubs of America, 17
Due Process Clause and due process of law, xiv, 23ff.

Eighteenth Amendment, 36
Eighth Amendment, 38
England, 4, 5, 14, 31
equal protection clause, 30–1

Federalist Papers, 19
Fetus, 3
Fifth Amendment, 23, 27, 31, 33, 37, 38, 39, 42, 57; see also double jeopardy, Due Process Clause, Self-Incrimination Clause
First Amendment, xiii, xiv, 7, 17, 18, 38, 43ff.
Founding Fathers: see Framers
Fourteenth Amendment, xiii, 10, 23, 25, 34, 35, 36, 38, 39, 42, 46, 48, 53; see also Due Process Clause

Fourth Amendment, 9–10, 26, 38
Framers, 4, 5, 9, 10, 19, 45, 55
Franklin, Benjamin, 22; quoted, 21

Goldberg, Arthur, 40; quoted, 62

Hamilton, Alexander, 6
Harding, Warren G., 40–1
Harlan, John Marshall, xi
Holdsworth, William S., xii
Holmes, Oliver Wendell, 39; quoted, 26 and n., 28 and n.
House Un-American Activities Committee, 50
Howard, Dick, 33

James II, 4
Jefferson, Thomas, 6, 11, 48 and n., 49 and n.
John, King of England, 32
judges, power and, 12ff.; see also Due Process Clause, judicial activism
judicial activism, xiv, 14–15, 20–1
judicial restraint, xiv, 18–22
judicial review, 19
jury trial, rules for constitutional fair, 33, 34, 35, 36

Levellers, 6, 32 and n.
libel laws, 48, 53

Lilburne, John, 4 and *n.*, 5 and *n.*

Madison, James, 6, 7, 21*n.*, 45; quoted, 19, 22 and *n.*
Magna Carta, 31–3, 45
Marshall, John: quoted, 18–19
Miller, Samuel F., xv
Mormonism, and polygamy, 55–6

"natural law," 35, 36
Necessary and Proper Clause, 9
North Briton, The (newspaper), 13 and *n.*

obscenity laws, 47, 48, 53

Paul, 4
"peacable assembly," right of, 45
petition, freedom of, 50, 58
picketing and demonstration, 54–5, 56–7, 59
pledge of allegiance, and First and Fourteenth Amendments, xiii
Pliny, 3
Pollock, Frederick, xiii
polygamy, and Mormonism, 55–6

press, freedom of, 43, 45, 50, 57, 58
privacy, right of, 9–10

racial discrimination, 60
Reconstruction, 65
religion, freedom of, 43–4, 45

Self-Incrimination Clause, 5, 6, 38, 39
Seventh Amendment, 36
Ship Money cases, 12–13
"shock-the-conscience" test of constitutionality, 23, 28–31
Sixth Amendment, 38
speech, freedom of, 16–17, 18, 43, 44, 45–63
states' rights, 37, 40, 60
"Statute for Religious Liberty," 53
Story, Joseph, xv
Subversive Activities Control Act, 64 Stat. 987–1005, 50 U. S. C. §§781–798 (1964), 16
Subversive Activities Control Board, 16, 17, 18

Taft, William H., 40–1
Trajan, 3

Udall, John, 5 and *n.*

University of Virginia Law
School, 33
"unreasonableness" of statutes
and constitutionality, 23,
24, 26, 28, 33, 35, 38
Utah Territory, 56

Washington, George, 6
Wilkes, John, 13
Wilson, Justice, xv

Yale Review, 40 and *n.*

A Note About the Author

HUGO LAFAYETTE BLACK was born in Harlan, Alabama, on February 27, 1886. He was awarded the LL.B., University of Alabama, 1906, then went into practice in Ashland, Alabama, in 1906, and in Birmingham, Alabama, in 1907. He was Police Judge, 1910–11, and Prosecuting Attorney of Jefferson County, Alabama, 1915–17. After military service, 1917–18, he returned to general practice in Birmingham, 1919–27. In 1926 he was elected United States Senator and was re-elected in 1932. He was President Franklin D. Roosevelt's first Supreme Court appointee, in 1937. Senior Justice since 1946, he has served more than thirty years. He was married in 1921 to Josephine Foster; they had two sons and a daughter. In 1957, five years after his first wife's death, he married Elizabeth Seay DeMeritte. They live in Alexandria, Virginia.

A Note on the Type

The text of this book has been set on the Monotype in a type-face called "Baskerville." The face is a facsimile reproduction of type cast from molds made for JOHN BASKERVILLE (1706–1775) from his designs. The punches for the revived Linotype Baskerville were cut under the supervision of the English printer George W. Jones.

The original face by John Baskerville was one of the forerunners of the type-style known as "modern face" to printers: a "modern" of the period A.D. 1800.

The book was composed, printed, and bound
by The Haddon Craftsmen, Inc.,
Scranton, Pennsylvania
Typography and binding design by Janet Gasson

Date Due

Mar 10			
MAR 1 3 1969			
Feb 20 '72			
Mar 10 72			
O C 5 '72			
Oct 30 75			